COLOR YOUR OWN
ABSTRACT ART
MASTERPIECES

Muncie Hendler

DOVER PUBLICATIONS, INC.
Mineola, New York

NOTE

Manipulating color, shape, and brushstroke, abstract artists relied on the basic elements of art to provide the only avenue of communication in their work. Appreciation of early abstract art was hindered by the prevailing notion that a subject was imperative to a painting. However, abstract artists firmly rejected this idea and eliminated all of the intrinsic "distractions" of a subject, exposing only the pure forms.

Predominant twentieth-century modern art styles, including Fauvism, Cubism, Expressionism, and Futurism, spawned an increased fervor for abstracted representations of the physical world. Abstract art, in turn, inspired offshoots in such subcategories as Abstract Expressionism, Minimalism, and Precisionism, all executed on very large canvases. More than an energetic and powerful emotional style, Abstract Expressionism was an artistic philosophy emphasizing color and detailed brushstrokes.

Minimal art, finding a niche during the 1960s, simplified composition even further. Line, shape, and color—the pure forms of Minimalism—generated a reality that was based solely on geometric relationships. The Constructivism movement in Russia was a major influence on geometric abstraction. Often misconstrued as a limitation, this reductionist technique did not impede the growth of abstract art, since artists adapted a variety of approaches, thereby individualizing their work. One approach involved loose, active brushstrokes yielding lyrical, fluid shapes, while another was more structured, devoting canvases to a variety of geometric shapes with mathematical precision. Applying thin paint to the canvas—without any visible brushstrokes—achieved the effect of solid color. Minimalist painter Frank Stella even altered the shape of his canvases to mesh with his lines and forms.

Included in this unique collection are the works of nineteen different abstract artists. Essential relationships between form and color may be altered simply by changing the colors used in each painting. Notice how the tone of the painting is affected by hue. Color renditions of the original paintings are reproduced on the inside covers if you want to follow the artists' color schemes. Captions identify the artist, title of the work, date of composition, and the medium employed.

Bibliographical Note

Color Your Own Abstract Art Masterpieces is a new work, first published by Dover Publications, Inc., in 1999.

DOVER *Pictorial Archive* SERIES

This book belongs to the Dover Pictorial Archive Series. You may use the designs and illustrations for graphics and crafts applications, free and without special permission, provided that you include no more than four in the same publication or project. (For permission for additional use, please write to Permissions Department, Dover Publications, Inc., 31 East 2nd Street, Mineola, N.Y. 11501.)
However, republication or reproduction of any illustration by any other graphic service, whether it be in a book or in any other design resource, is strictly prohibited.

International Standard Book Number: 0-486-40800-0

Manufactured in the United States of America
Dover Publications, Inc., 31 East 2nd Street, Mineola, N.Y. 11501

1.   Stuart Davis (1894–1964). *Hot Still-Scape for Six Colors—Seventh Avenue Style*, 1940. Oil on canvas.

2. **Stuart Davis** (1894–1964). *Owh! in San Pao,* 1951. Oil on canvas.

3.   **Stuart Davis** (1894–1964). *Medium Still Life,* 1953. Oil on canvas.

4.   **Ad Reinhardt** (1913–1967). *Number 30*, 1938. Oil on canvas.

5. Adolph Gottlieb (1903–1974). *The Seer*, 1950. Oil on canvas.

6.   Patrick Henry Bruce (1881–1936). *Forms (Peinture)*, c. 1919–20. Oil on canvas.

7. **Patrick Henry Bruce** (1881–1936). *Painting*, c. 1921–22. Oil on canvas.

8.   **Marsden Hartley** (1877–1943). *The Aero*, 1914. Oil on canvas.

9.   **Marsden Hartley** (1877–1943). *Painting No. 2*, 1914. Oil on canvas.

10.   **Kenneth Noland** (1924–   ). *Beginning*, 1958. Acrylic on canvas.

11. **Kenneth Noland** (1924–). *Bend Sinister*, 1964. Acrylic on canvas.

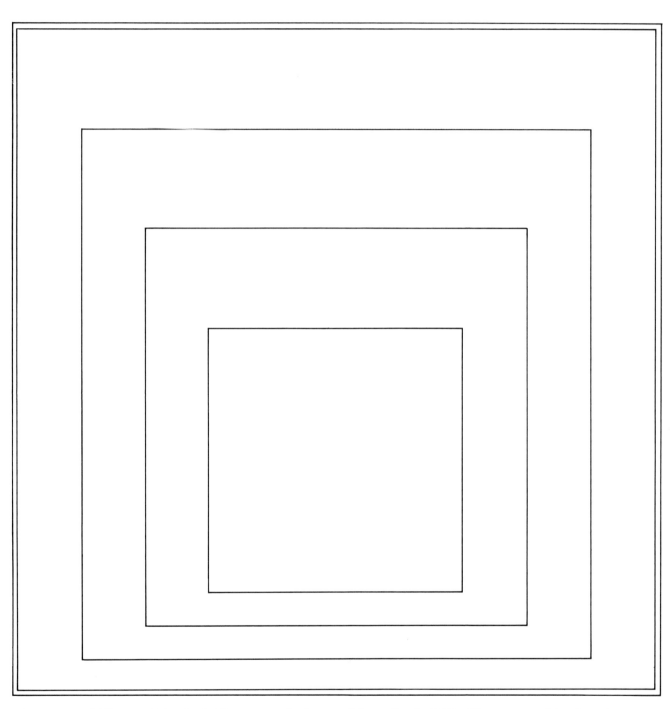

12.　　**Josef Albers** (1888–1976). *Homage to the Square: "Ascending"*, 1953. Oil on composition board.

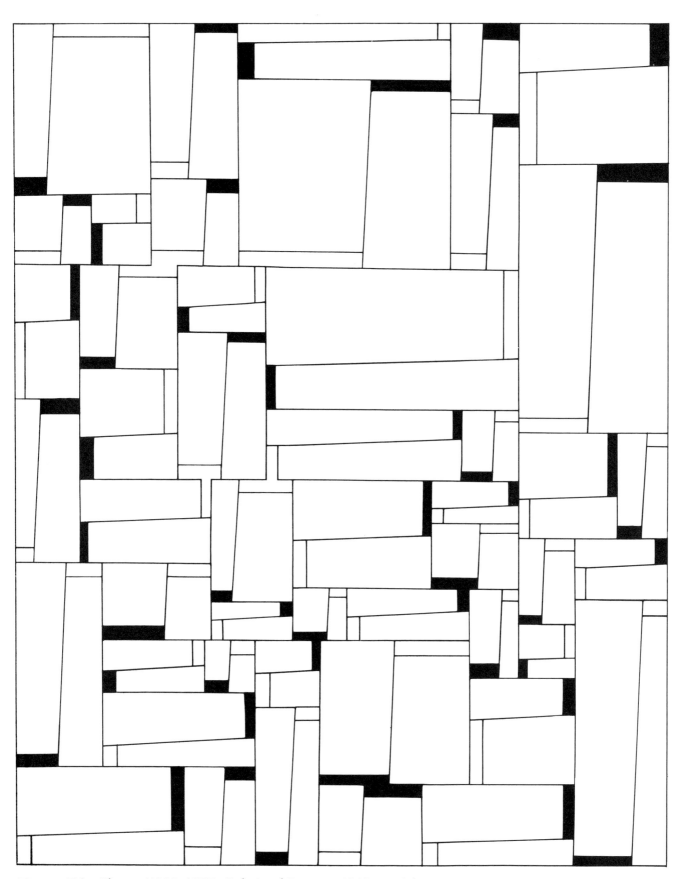

13.   **Fritz Glarner** (1899–1972). *Relational Painting*, 1949–51. Oil on canvas.

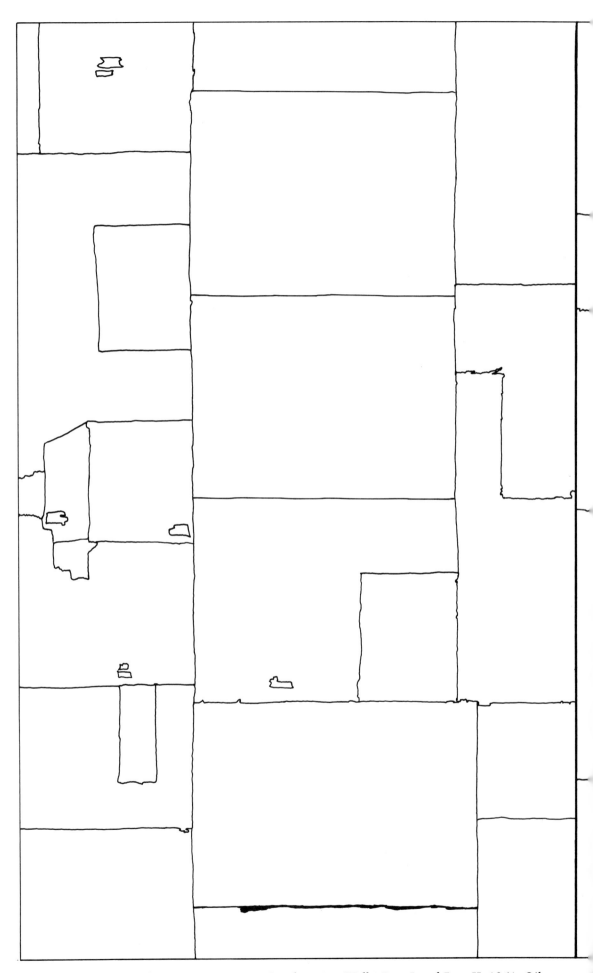

14–15.   **Hans Hofmann** (1880–1966). *Combination Wall—Part I and Part II*, 1961. Oil on canv

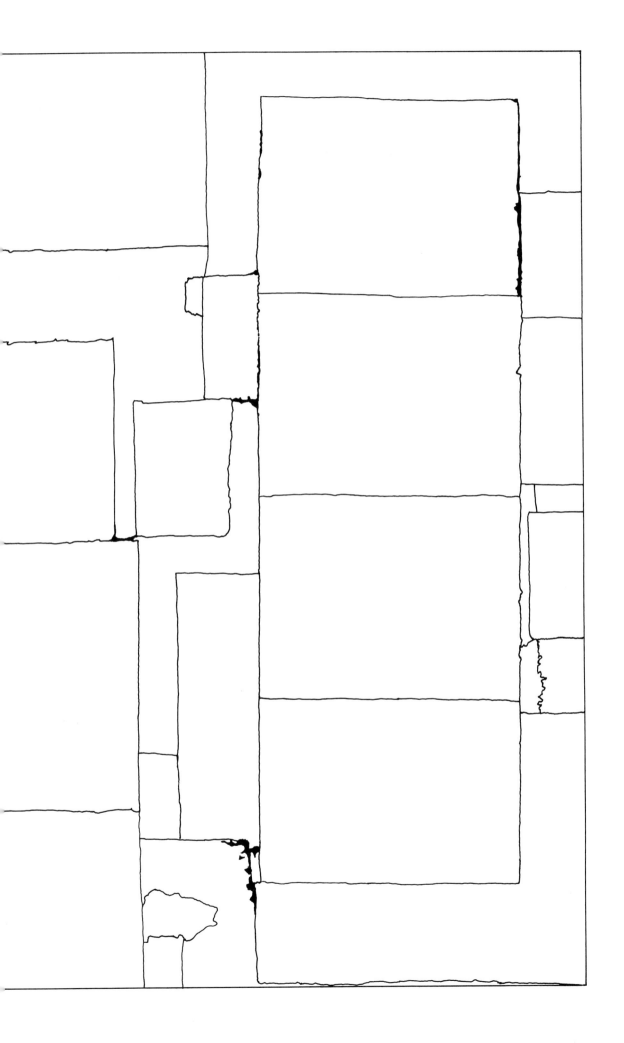

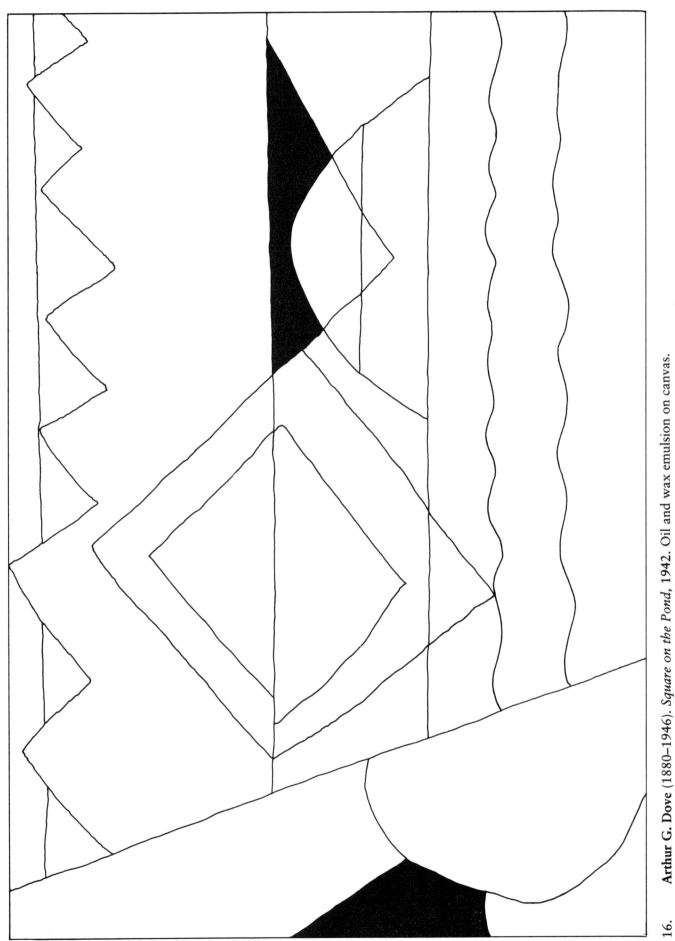

16.   **Arthur G. Dove** (1880–1946). *Square on the Pond*, 1942. Oil and wax emulsion on canvas.

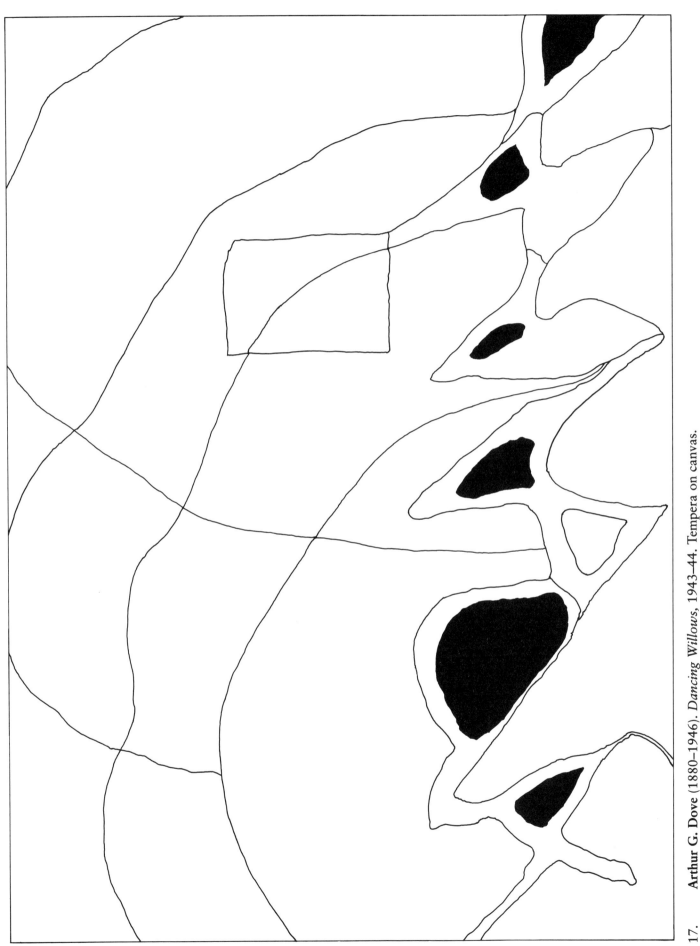

17. **Arthur G. Dove** (1880–1946). *Dancing Willows*, 1943–44. Tempera on canvas.

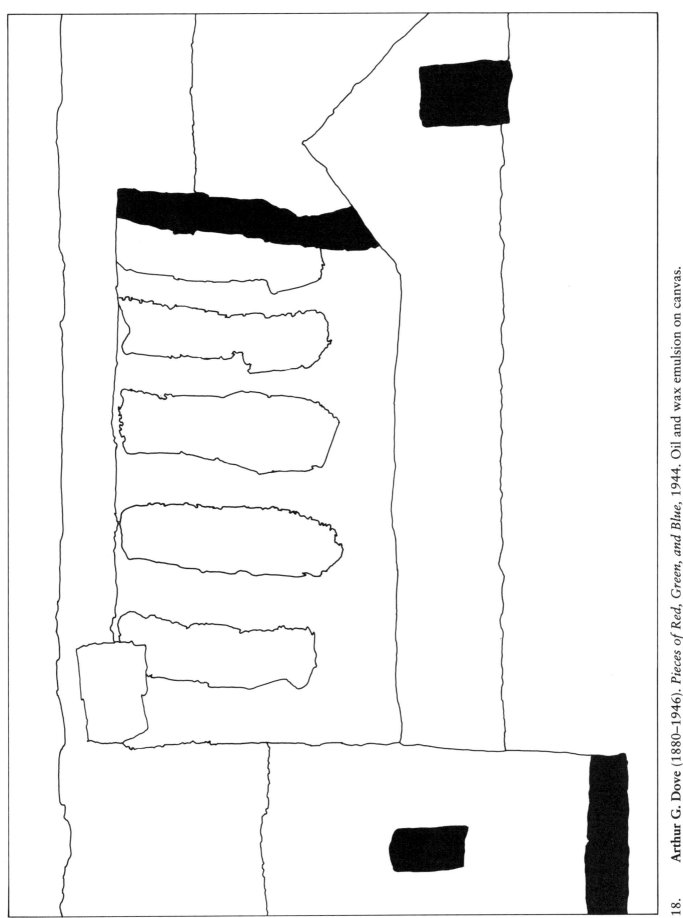

18. **Arthur G. Dove** (1880–1946). *Pieces of Red, Green, and Blue*, 1944. Oil and wax emulsion on canvas.

19. Morris Louis (1912–1962). *Alpha*, 1960. Acrylic resin paint on canvas.

20.   **Frank Stella** (1936–   ). *Darabjerd III*, 1967. Fluorescent acrylic on canvas.

21.   **Frank Stella** (1936–   ). *Lac Laronge III*, 1969. Polymer paint on canvas.

22.   **Frank Stella** (1936–   ). *Pilicia II*, 1973. Relief collage of mixed media.

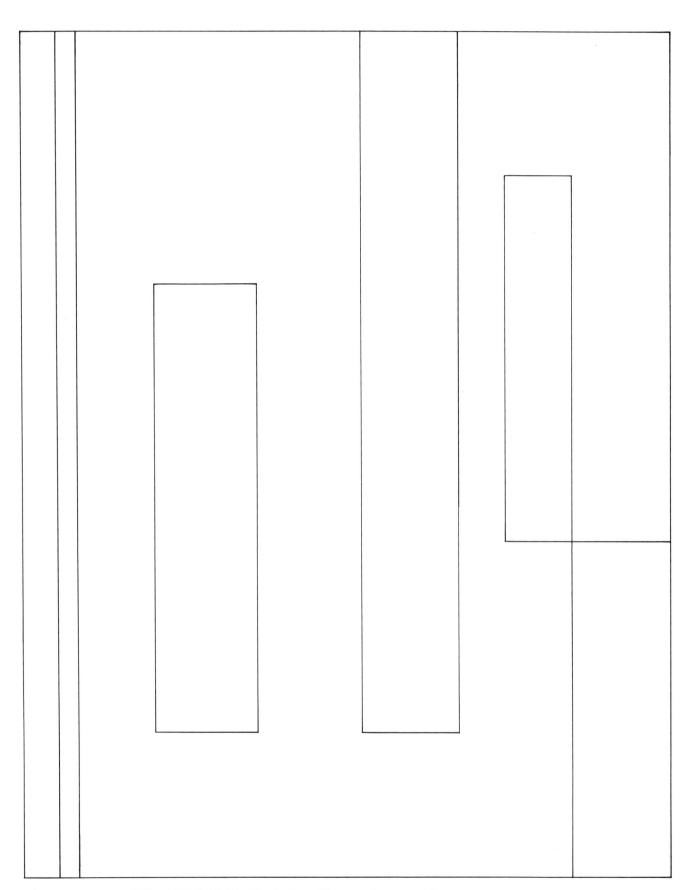

23.   **Burgoyne Diller** (1906–1965). *No. 2, First Theme*, 1955–60. Oil on canvas.

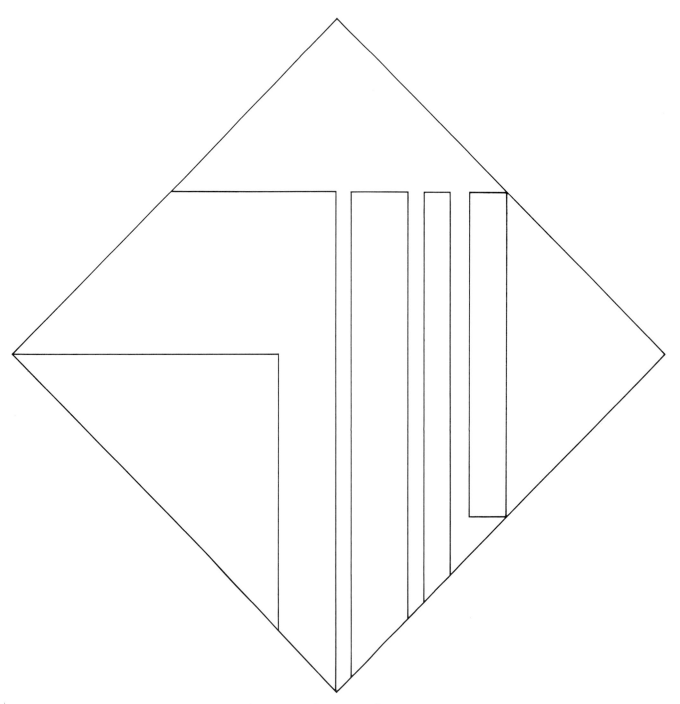

24.   **Ilya Bolotowsky** (1907–   ). *Scarlet Diamond,* 1969. Oil on canvas.

25.   **Helen Frankenthaler** (1928–   ). *Indian Summer,* 1967. Acrylic on canvas.

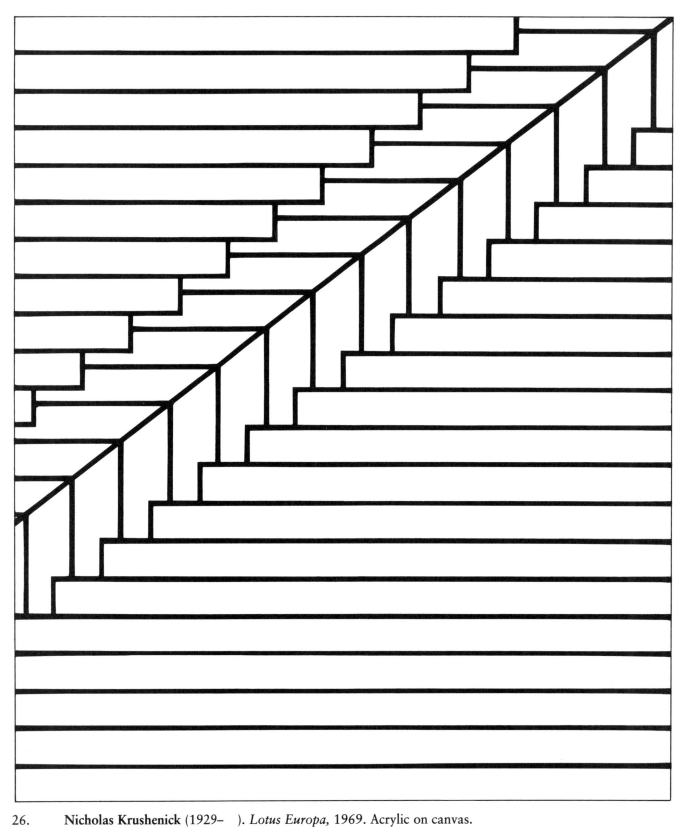

26.   **Nicholas Krushenick** (1929–   ). *Lotus Europa,* 1969. Acrylic on canvas.

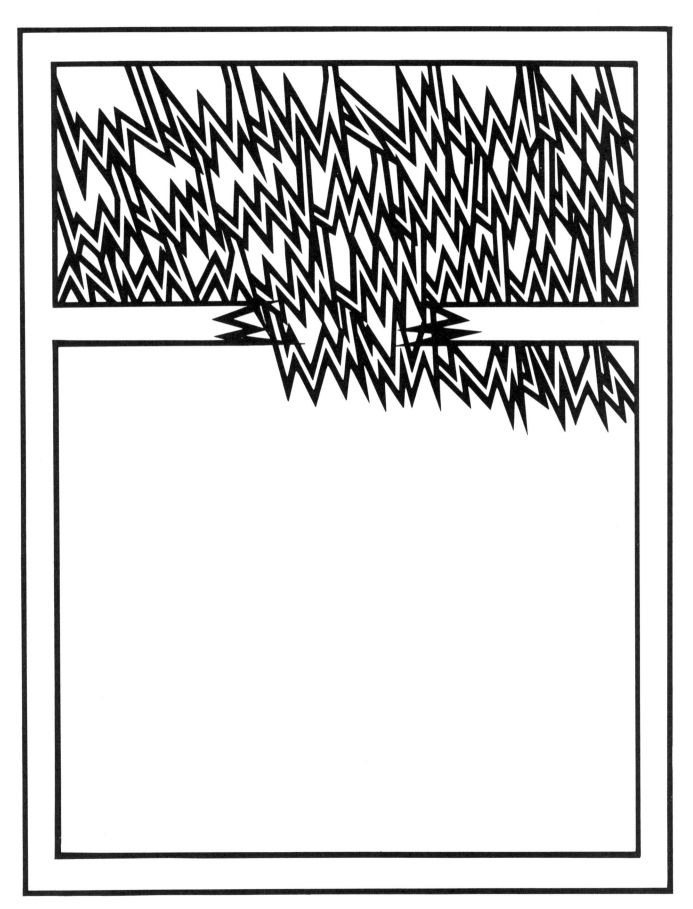

27.   **Nicholas Krushenick** (1929–   ). *Measure of Red,* 1971. Acrylic on canvas.

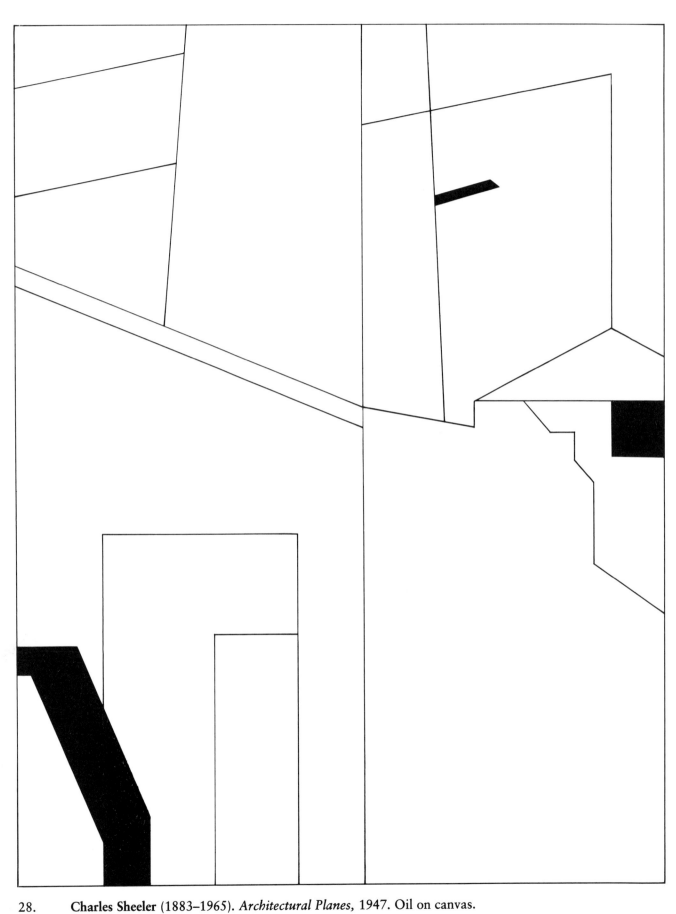

28.   **Charles Sheeler** (1883–1965). *Architectural Planes,* 1947. Oil on canvas.

29.   **Niles Spencer** (1893–1952). *Above the Excavation,* 1950. Oil on canvas.

30.   **Larry Zox** (1936–   ). *Diamond Drill Series—Trobriand,* 1967. Acrylic and epoxy on canvas.